Written by Jill Wolf • Illustrated by J. Corbitt

ISBN 0-89954-950-0
Made in the United States of America

Antioch Publishing Company
Yellow Springs, Ohio 45387

Why don't ducks like to get mail?

They already have bills.

Knock knock.
Who's there?
Quack.
Quack who?

Quack the door open so you can hear me better!

What do you get if you cross
a duck and a kettle?
A quackpot.

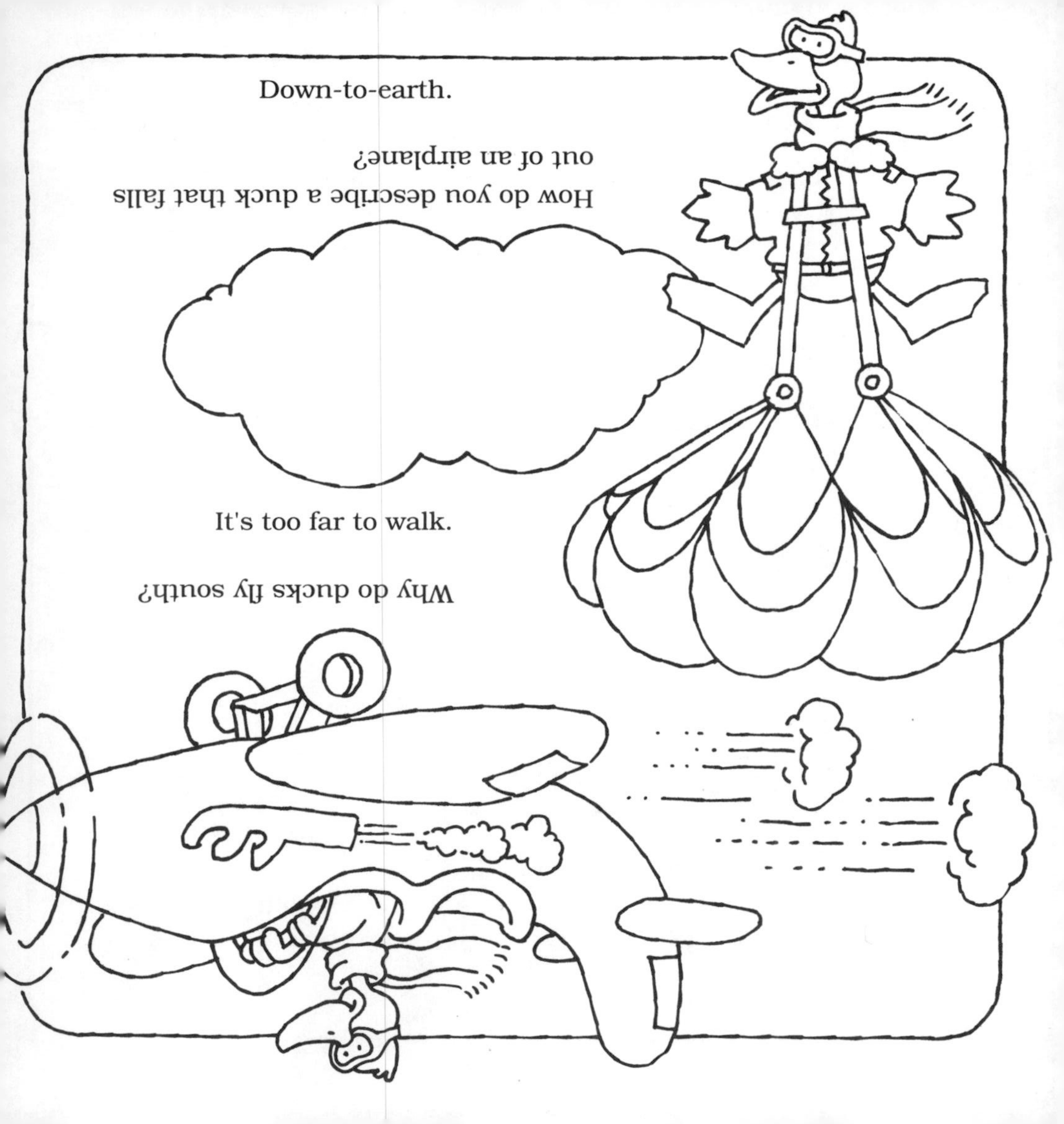
Why do ducks fly south?
It's too far to walk.
How do you describe a duck that falls
out of an airplane?
Down-to-earth.

How can you tell when a duck
thinks something is funny?
It quacks up.

Why did the cook put
suntan oil on the duck?
He wanted all dark meat.
Why does a duck never swim
on an empty stomach?
It's easier to swim in water.

What kind of jokes does a duck make?

Wisequacks.

What do you get if you cross a duck and a dinosaur?
I don't know, but when it quacks, everyone listens!
QUACK!
When won't a duck fight?
If it's chicken.

What do ducks do at Christmas?
They put duck-orations on their Christmas trees.

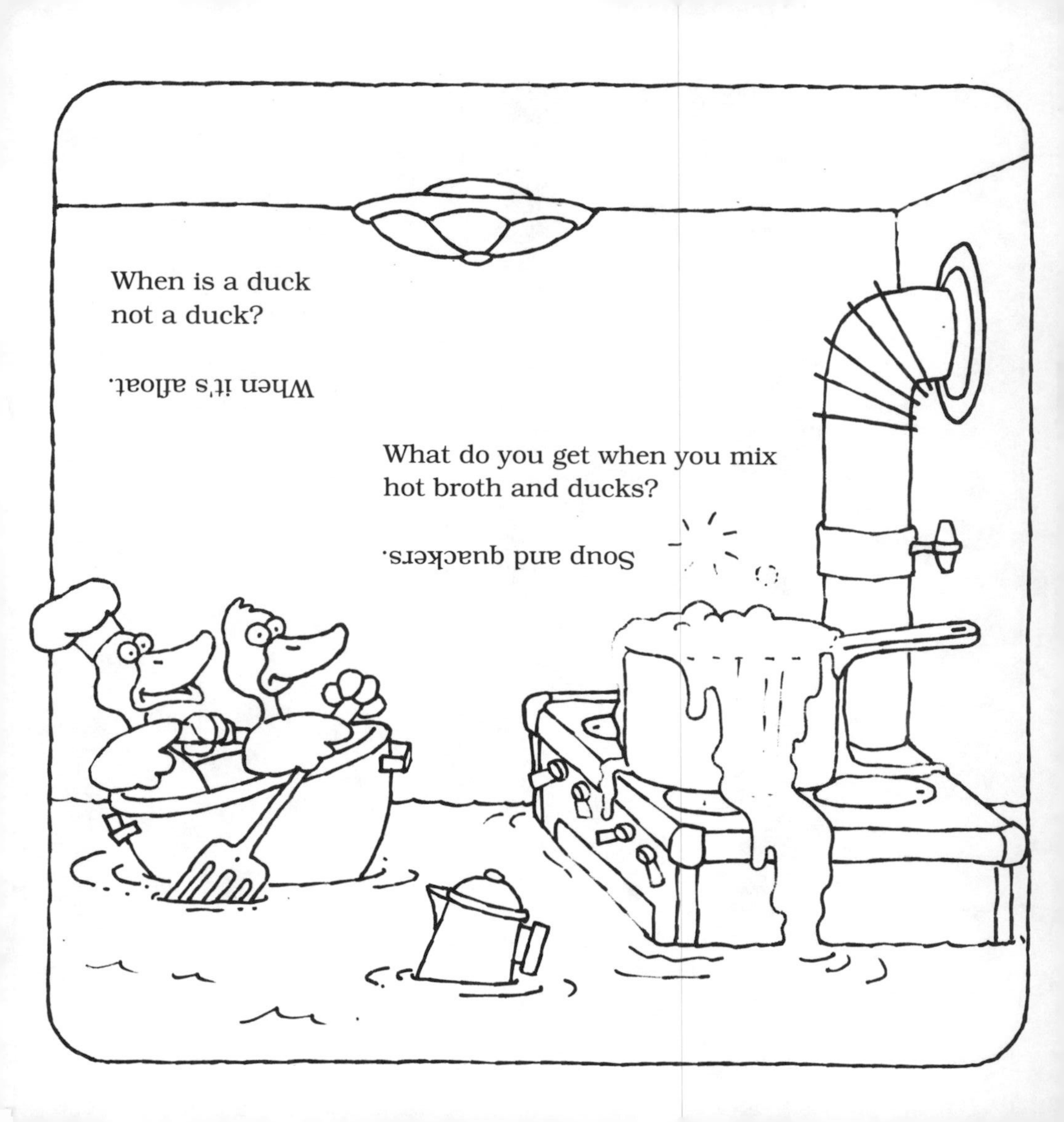

When is a duck
not a duck?

When it's afloat.

What do you get when you mix
hot broth and ducks?

Soup and quackers.

Why did the duck feel silly when it sang rock 'n' roll?

Because its voice quacked.

What did the doctor give the duck?
A clean bill of health.
What do you call a person
who keeps ducks?
A bill collector.
DUCKTOR
WOBERTS

What duck has feathers, wings, and fangs?
Count Drake-cula.
What has 3 feet, 3 eyes, and 2 bills?
A duck with spare parts.

What duck breaks
into a bank vault?

A safequacker.

What do you call it
when a detective
duck solves a mystery?

A brilliant de-duck-tion.

What does a duck
wear to a wedding?
A ducks-edo.

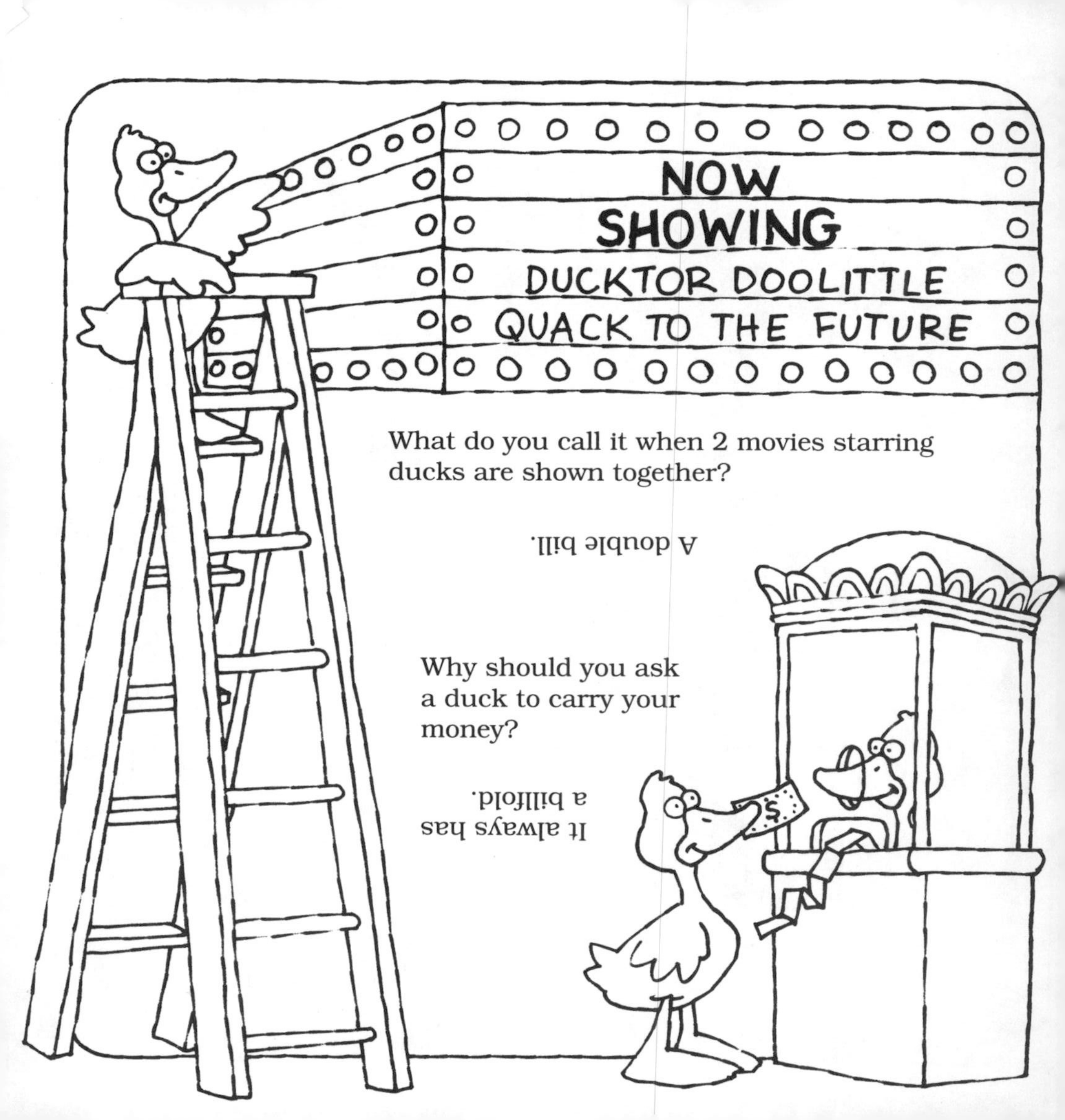

What do you call it when 2 movies starring ducks are shown together?

A double bill.

Why should you ask a duck to carry your money?

It always has a billfold.

What goes "QUACK-QUACK!"
and weighs 20,000 pounds?
King Kong Duck.

If he wants to catch a duck, what does a ship's captain say to his crew?

"All hands on duck!"

What did the duck say to the
salesclerk when it bought lipstick?
"Just put it on my bill."

Where do ducks advertise?

On a billboard.

What happens when ducks fly upside down?

They quack up.

What do you call a duck
with a cherry bomb?

A firequacker.

What do you get when you cross a duck with a can of cola?

A soda quacker.

Why aren't ducks good baseball players?

They always hit fowl balls.

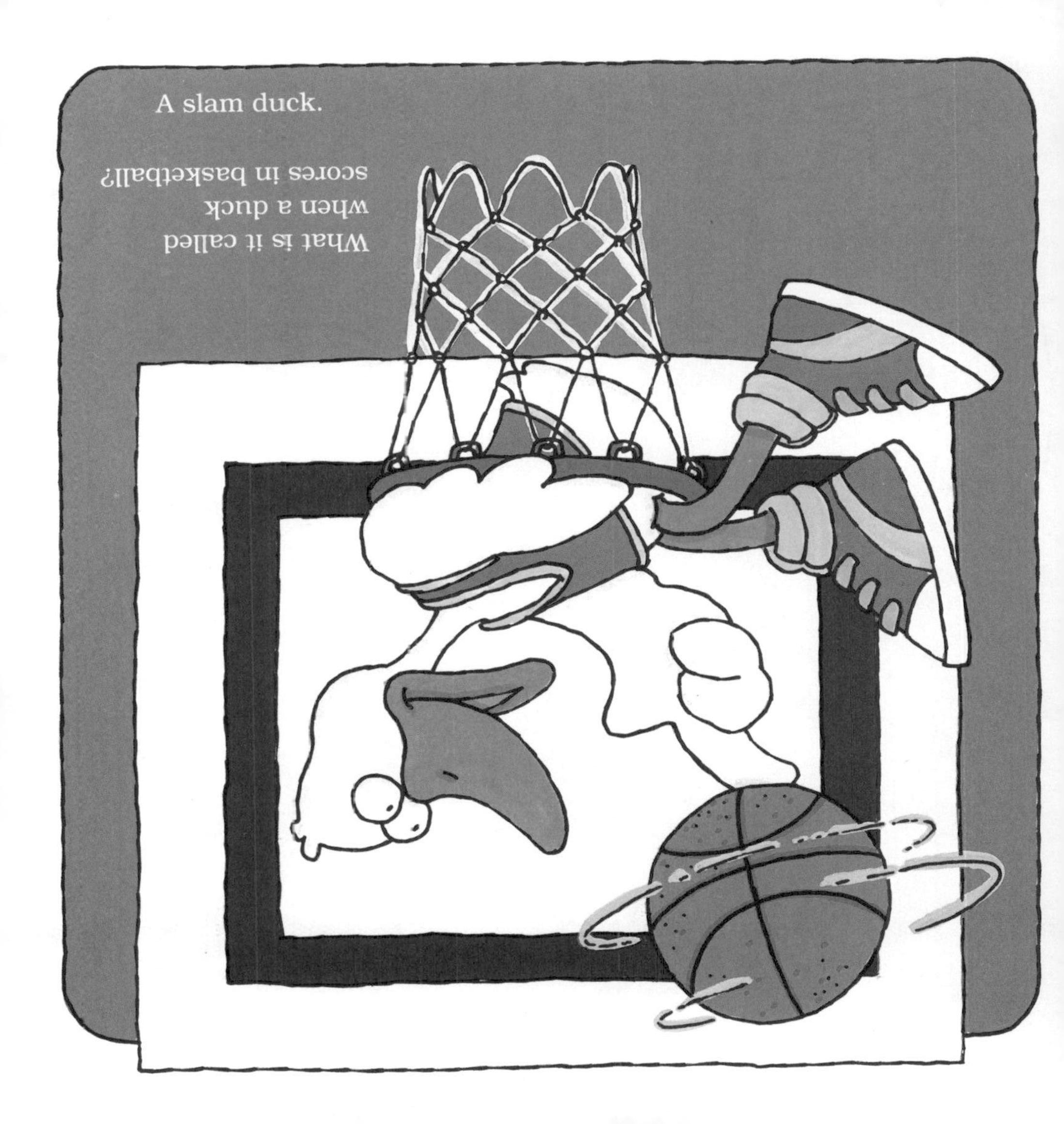
What is it called
when a duck
scores in basketball?
A slam duck.

What do you call a news
show about ducks?

A duck-umentary.

What do you call a duck
in a bean bag chair?

A sitting duck.